Collins
INTERNATIONAL PRIMARY ENGLISH

T0312476

Student's Book 1

William Collins' dream of knowledge for all began with the publication of his first book in 1819. A self-educated mill worker, he not only enriched millions of lives, but also founded a flourishing publishing house. Today, staying true to this spirit, Collins books are packed with inspiration, innovation and practical expertise. They place you at the centre of a world of possibility and give you exactly what you need to explore it.

Collins. Freedom to teach.

Published by Collins
An imprint of HarperCollins*Publishers*
The News Building
1 London Bridge Street
London SE1 9GF

HarperCollins*Publishers*, Macken House, 39/40 Mayor Street Upper, Dublin 1, DO1 C9W8, Ireland

Browse the complete Collins catalogue at
www.collins.co.uk

ISBN 978-0-00-834088-9

British Library Cataloguing-in-Publication Data
A catalogue record for this publication is available from the British Library.

Author: Joyce Vallar
Series editor: Daphne Paizee
Publisher: Elaine Higgleton
Product developer: Natasha Paul
Project manager: Karen Williams
Development editor: Sonya Newland
Copyeditor: Karen Williams
Proofreader: Catherine Dakin
Cover designer: Gordon MacGilp

Cover illustrator: Petr Horácek
Internal designer and typesetter: Ken Vail Graphic Design Ltd.
Text permissions researcher: Rachel Thorne
Image permissions researcher: Alison Prior
Illustrators: Ken Vail Graphic Design Ltd., Advocate Art, Beehive Illustration and QBS Learning
Production controller: Lyndsey Rogers
Printed in Great Britain by Martins the Printers

Third-party websites, publications and resources referred to in this publication have not been endorsed by Cambridge Assessment International Education.

With thanks to the following teachers and schools for reviewing materials in development: Amanda DuPratt, Shreyaa Dutta Gupta, Sharmila Majumdar, Sushmita Ray and Sukanya Singhal, Calcutta International School; Akash Raut, DSB International School, Mumbai; Melissa Brobst, International School of Budapest; Shalini Reddy, Manthan International School; Taman Rama Intercultural School.

Contents

How to use this book

- **Key texts and images**
  The texts in Stage 1 provide a wide variety of different genres for learners to enjoy. The colourful illustrations provide enjoyment as well as essential support for learners as they learn to read. Learners are introduced to stories by published authors and a variety of illustration styles.

- **Remember boxes**
  These are used to remind learners to do things that they have already learned, such as the correct use of punctuation marks.

Remember!
Use capital letters at the beginning of names of people and places.

- **Word book**
  These are introduced in Unit 7 in Stage 1 and are used throughout this course. Word books allow learners to compile their own personal dictionaries which they can refer to in their writing activities. They also help learners to develop dictionary skills.

Word book

Write the words from question 2 in your Word book.

- **Thinking time**
  These occur at the end of each unit in the Student's Book. Learners are encouraged to reflect on what they have read, listened to, discussed and learned.

Thinking time

Which did you prefer, *Bot on the Moon* or *Mister Moon*? Why?

1 Going places

Listening and speaking

Listen. Then answer the questions.

- How do you go to school?
- Where do you like to play?
- Where do you go shopping?
- Where is your favourite place to play?

Vocabulary: transport words

1 **Look at the pictures. Read the words.**

bicycle

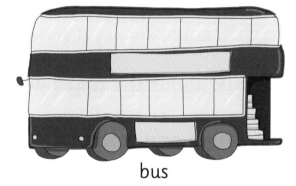

bus

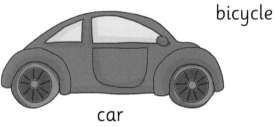

car

truck

2 **Answer the questions.**

- What colour is the bus?
- What colour is the truck?
- How many wheels does the bicycle have?
- How many wheels does a car have?

3 **Draw and label some other types of transport.**

Listening and speaking

1 **Listen to the poem.**

> On the bus
> All six of us
> On we hop
> We sit at the top
> Up and down
> Into town
> Off we get
> Oh no! We're not there yet!

The Big Red Bus

Alison Hawes   Woody Fox

2 **Talk about the times when you go on a bus.**

Reading and writing

Look at the cover of the book at the top of this page.
- What is the book called?
- What does the title tell you about the bus?
- What do you think the book will be about?

Listening and speaking

1 **PAIR WORK. Listen to the story. Think about the questions.**
- Where is the bus going?
- Who is waiting for the girl when she gets off the bus?

2 **Take turns to read the story.**

3 **Ask and answer questions about the story.**

The Big Red Bus

A big red bus is at the bus stop.

It is the bus to Nut Hill.

We get on the bus.

We get a trip to Nut Hill.

We sit at the back of the bus.

The bus is fast.

We grab on to the rail.

We pass the pond and the clock.

We get to Nut Hill at last.

I press the bell to get off.

Grandad is at the bus stop.

I run up and hug him.

Read the sentences. Say which ones are true.
Copy the true sentences.

- The bus is going to Nut Hill.
- The bus is very slow.
- The bus went past the pond.
- You press the bell to get off.

1 Read each word aloud. Listen to the beginning sound of each word.

bag　map　cap　mix　man　bus　cot　can　bed

2 Write the words in lists, like the example below.

c words	**b** words	**m** words
cap		

3 Look at the pictures. Say what they show. Write the words.

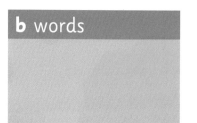

Reading and speaking

PAIR WORK. Take turns to tell the story in your own words. Use the story map to help you.

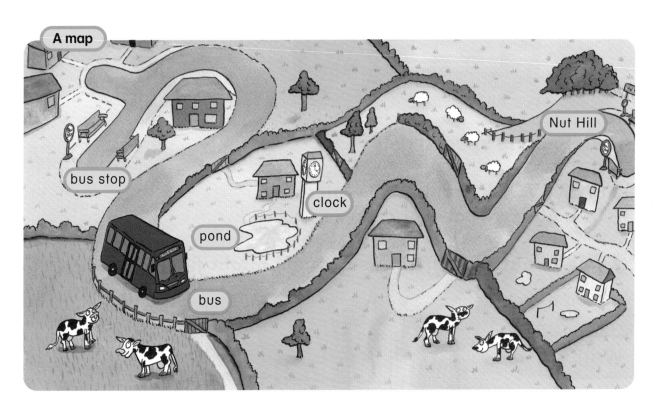

A map

bus stop

Nut Hill

clock

pond

bus

Reading and writing

1. Read the sentences in the purple box. Find the sentences in the story.

2. Write the sentence which is at the beginning of the story.

We pass the pond and the clock.

We get on the bus.

Grandad is at the bus stop.

We sit at the back of the bus.

3. Write the other sentences in the correct order.

Reading and speaking

1 PAIR WORK. **Look at the picture. Talk about what you can see.**

2 **Talk about the different signs you might find:**

- on a shop door.
- in a shop window.

Writing

1 PAIR WORK. **Make a sign for:**

- a shop door.
- a shop window.

2 **Make a list of different types of shoes. Read your list to a partner.**

Role play

1 PAIR WORK. **What do you say when you are in a shop and you want to buy new shoes?**

2 **Act out what happens in the shoe shop. Take turns to be the shopkeeper and the shopper.**

Reading and writing

1 Write captions for each picture.

This is the café.

2 Look at the pictures of things people can buy.
Say the word for each picture. Write the words.

Reading

1 **Look at the book covers. Read the titles.**

2 **Answer the questions.**

- Which book is a story book? How do you know?
- Which book did Becca Heddle write?
- In which book can you find out about cats?
- Which book would you like to read? Say why.

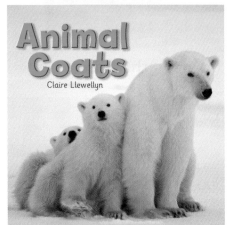

3 **Find a book in the class library that:**

- tells a story.
- gives information about animals.

4 **Write the titles of the books that you found.**

Thinking time

Talk about *The Big Red Bus*.
Did you enjoy the story?
Did you like the pictures?

2 Having fun

PAIR WORK. Talk about what you do to keep fit.

- What do you do to keep fit?
- What is your favourite thing to do to keep fit?
- Do you exercise alone or with friends?
- What sport would you like to be able to do?

Rev and Dev

By
Joyce Vallar

Illustrated by
Madhavi Poddar

Reading and writing

Look at the book cover.

- What is the title of the book?
- What do you think the book is about?

Reading and listening

Listen to the story.

- What do you notice about the way the story is written?
- What does Dev like doing?
- What does Rev like doing?

Rev and Dev

1

Rev and Dev like to play in the sun.
Rev and Dev like to run and have fun.

2

Rev said to Dev, "What can you do?
Show me, show me, what can you do?"

3

"I can run for fun.
I can run to get fit.
I can run in the sun.
Then sit for a bit."

4

Dev said to Rev, "Can you run like me?
Show me, show me, what can you do?"

5

"I can run for fun
with a cap and a map.
I can run in the sun
with a bag and a rag."

6

Rev said to Dev, "What more
can you do?

Show me, show me, what more
can you do?"

7

"I can hop for a bit.
I can hop to get fit.
I can hop on the top
of a box and then sit."

8

Dev said to Rev, "Can you hop
like me?

Show me, show me, what can
you do?"

9

"I can hop for a bit.
I can hop to get fit.
I can hop on a rug
with a jug and a mug."

10

Rev said to Dev, "What more
can you do?

Show me, show me, what more
can you do?"

11

"I can jog with my frog
and a fish on a dish.
I can jog in the mud.
Oops! I'm down with a thud!"

12

Rev said to Dev, "I can do that!
Yes <u>we</u> can have fun in the mud
in the sun!"

1 PAIR WORK. Read the story out loud. Write the names of the two characters in the story.

2 Tell your partner two things from the story that Rev likes doing and two things that Dev likes doing.

Vocabulary: action words

1 Look at the pictures. Read the words.

> **Remember!**
> Action words are called verbs, for example 'hop', 'sit'.
> Words that are the names of things are nouns, for example 'box', 'cap'.

sitting

running

jogging

hopping

2 Answer the questions about Rev and Dev.

- Who can hop on the top of a box and then sit?
- Who can run for fun with a cap and a map?
- Who can hop with a jug and a mug?
- Who can jog in the mud?

Spelling: high-frequency words

1 **Read each word aloud.**

said   you   with   the

- Find the words in the story, *Rev and Dev*.
- Write the words in a list. Use tally marks to show how many of each word you find.

said	~~HHH~~ /
you	
with	
the	

2 **Write the sentences. Use the words from the box.**

on   and   my   for

- I can run _____ fun.
- I can hop with a jug _____ a mug.
- I can hop _____ top of a box.
- I can jog with _____ frog.

Speaking and writing

1 PAIR WORK. Talk about what sports the children are doing.

2 Choose one sport and tell your partner about it.

3 Draw a picture and write a caption for your sport.

Sounds and spelling

1 Read each word aloud. Listen to the sound at the end of each word.

bag   leg   log   peg   wag   frog

- Write the pairs of words that rhyme.
- Which word does not have a rhyming partner?

2 Make groups of rhyming words.

ſ + ix   w + ax   b + ox   t + ax

m + ix   s + ix   f + ox

3 Draw and label pictures for 'six', 'box' and 'fox'.

Sounds and spelling

Look at the pictures and say what they show.
Write the pairs of words that rhyme.

Writing

My name is Rev.

My name is Dev.

Remember!
Use capital letters at the beginning of names of people and places.

1 Write a list of names of six people in your class.

2 Look at the alphabet.

A B C D E F G H I J K L M N O P Q R S T U V W X Y Z
    Dev   Jack   Rev

- Write the letter of the alphabet that your name starts with.
- Is the letter near the beginning, the middle or the end of the alphabet?

Read *Rev and Dev* again. Read *The Big Red Bus* again.

- Work in pairs. Talk about the different ways the stories are written.
- Which way did you like best? Why?

Reading and writing

1 **Read pages 3, 5, 7, 9 and 11 of *Rev and Dev* again. Find rhyming words on each page. Write them in lists.**

Page 3   run   fit
          fun   sit
          sun   bit

2 **Read the sentences about Rev and Dev. Write the sentence that Rev said.**

I can jog with my frog
and a fish on a dish.

I can hop on a rug
with a jug and a mug.

I can hop on the top
of a box and then sit.

Reading and writing

1 Read about Dev. Write the words with a −*sh* at the end.

"I can jog with my frog and a fish on a dish."

2 Read the words in the clouds. Write three lists of rhyming words.

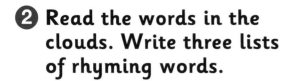

c + ash

f + ish

r + ush

h + ush

d + ish

m + ash

r + ash

w + ish

m + ush

Role play

PAIR WORK. Choose a page from the story to learn.

One person says, "Show me, show me what can you do?" The other says the next part with expression and actions. Then change roles.

Listening and speaking

PAIR WORK. Talk about what you have learned.

- How is the story written?
- How do you think Rev and Dev felt at the end of the story? What makes you think that?

Thinking time

What is your favourite way to exercise?

3 Let's find out

Listening and speaking

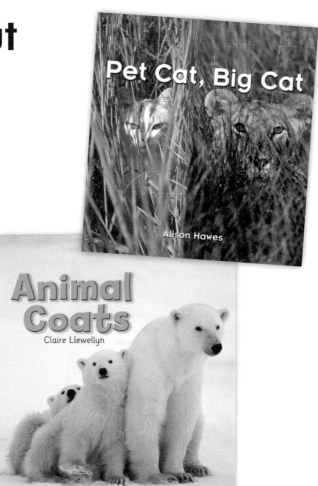

PAIR WORK. Look at the book covers. Talk about the books. Ask and answer questions like the ones below.

- What kind of books are they?
- What do you think each book is about?
- Which book would you use to find out about a snake's skin?
- Which book would you use to find out about lions?

Reading and writing

❶ Write the titles of the books.

❷ Write the title of a non-fiction book from your class library.

Reading and speaking

1 **PAIR WORK. Look at the pages from _Animal Coats_ below. What animal does it show?**

2 **Talk about what the pictures tell you about ducks.**

Who has a coat made of feathers?

duck

Reading and writing

Read the words in the box.

- Draw a picture of a duck and label it. Use the words in the box to help you.
- Write three sentences about ducks.

beak
wings
webbed feet
feathers

1 Look at the pictures. Say the word for each picture.
Write the words.

Sound it out

Two letters.
One sound: –**ng**

2 Write three more rhyming words.

d + ing   s + ing   p + ing

3 Look at the pictures. Say the word for each picture.
Write the words.

4 Write three more rhyming words.

d + ock   l + uck   b + ack
l + ock   s + uck   r + ack
r + ock   t + uck   p + ack

Sound it out

Two letters.
One sound: –**ck**

1 PAIR WORK. Look at the pages from *In the Forest*. Talk about what you might find in the forest.

This is a forest.

2 Draw and label an animal you might find in a forest.

3 Talk about these pictures.

4 Write a sentence about each picture.

Remember!
Capital letter at the beginning.
Full stop at the end.

Reading and writing

1 **Information books usually have a contents page. Read the contents page for a book about foxes.**

- Are these sentences?
- How do you know?

All About Foxes

Contents

2 **Answer the questions.**

- On what page would you find out about a fox's babies?
- On what page would you find out about what a fox eats?
- What would you find out about on page 12?
- What would you find out about on page 8?

Reading and speaking

PAIR WORK. Read the fact file about foxes. Say what you think you will learn about foxes.

Foxes eat almost anything, like berries, worms, spiders, mice and birds.

Foxes can live anywhere; in towns or in the countryside.

A fox's home is called a den.

FACT FILE: Foxes

Foxes go out mostly at night.

Foxes that live in a town or city sometimes eat trash from bins.

A baby fox is called a cub.

1 **Read about foxes in the fact file on page 26.**
Answer the questions.

- What is a fox's home called?
- Write the names of three things that a fox likes to eat.
- Where do foxes get food if they live in a town or city?
- What is a baby fox called?

2 **Look at the pictures. Read the captions.**
They show where we can find information.

in books

on the internet

by asking someone

3 **Find out what the young of these animals are called.**

4 **Write sentences like the one below.**

A baby tiger is called a...

Reading and writing

1 Use the pictures and labels to write three sentences about cats.

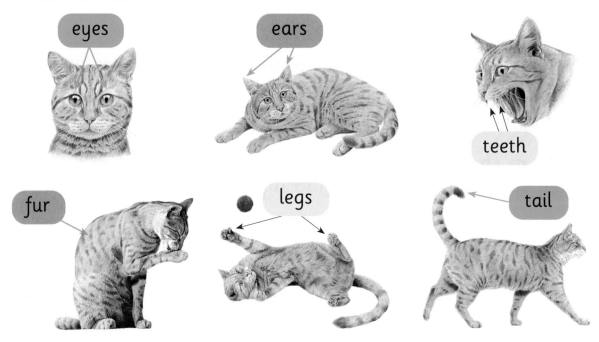

2 Look at the pictures. Read the words.
Make a list of the animals that belong to the cat family.

lion

owl

tiger

leopard

duck

snake

1 Read the rhyme. Answer the questions.

Five little ducks went swimming one day
Over the hills and far away
Mother duck said, "Quack, quack, quack, quack"
But only four little ducks came back.

- How many ducks went swimming?
- Write the pairs of rhyming words.

2 Write captions for the pictures.
Use the words in the box to help you.

one   two   three   four   five

1 Listen to a different poem about an animal. Listen for the rhyming words.

Lion by Giles Andreae

The lion's the king of the jungle,
Who quietly sits on his paws.
But everyone quivers
And shudders and shivers
As soon as he opens his jaws.

2 PAIR WORK. Take turns to read the poem.

3 Write the words that rhyme.

4 Write the names of three other animals you might find in a jungle.

5 Write two sentences for a fact file about one of the animals.

Thinking time

Which animals do you like and why?

4 The moon

PAIR WORK. Look at the book cover. Talk about it.

What do you think the book is about?
- Read the title.
- Look at the pictures.

31

Bot on the Moon

1

Bot was on a trip to the moon.

2

Blast off! Woosh!
His rocket was fast.
Zoom! Zoom! Zoom!

3

Bot zoomed past all the
twinkling stars.

4

Bot landed on the moon.
The moon was big. It had lots
of hills.

Bot ran up a hill and slid back to the foot of the hill.

He got a card and a moon rock at the Moon Shop.

He sent the card to his mum. It said, "Having a good trip. From Bot."

Bot got out the moon rock and his best golf club.

He hit the moon rock.
It was a big hit.
Bot let go of the club!

Bot had lost his club. He had to go back. Blast off! Zoom!

Bot was back with Mum.
He said, "I let go of my best club and I lost it."

Donk! Ow!
The club hit Bot on his hat.
The moon rock was back too!

Listen to the story. Think about the questions.

- How did Bot go to the moon?
- What did Bot buy in the Moon Shop?

Reading and writing

1 **PAIR WORK. Take turns to read *Bot on the Moon* out loud.**

2 **Answer the questions.**

- Was Bot's rocket fast or slow?
- What did Bot lose on the moon?

3 **Read the sentences. Write the sentences that are true.**

- The moon had lots of hills.
- Bot ran down the hill.
- Bot got a golf club at the Moon Shop.
- Bot had lost his club.
- The club hit Bot on his hat.

Speaking

PAIR WORK. Talk about what the moon is really like.

- Do people really play golf on the moon?
- Can you send a postcard from the moon?
- Can people go to the moon in a rocket?

1 **Read the sentences.**

Blast off! Woosh!
His rocket was fast.

2 **Read the words in the box. Write the words that rhyme with 'fast'.**

last   lost   past   nest   just   mast   fist

1 **Read page 4 of *Bot on the Moon* again.**

2 **How many sentences are on page 4?**

3 **Write the word that each sentence begins with.**

- What word does the first sentence begin with?
- What word does the second sentence begin with?
- What word does the last sentence begin with?

4 **Write a sentence about the moon.**

> Remember!
> Capital letters and full stops show us where sentences begin and end.

Sounds and spelling

1 **Look at the pictures. Say the words for each picture. Write the words.**

2 **Read the words in the box. Use the words to complete the sentences. Write the sentences.**

| got   and   the   _to_   He   his   the _____ |

_____ _____

- He _____ a card _____ a moon rock at _____ Moon Shop.
- _____ sent _____ card _____ mum.

Reading and writing

1 Draw a picture for a postcard that you would like to send from the moon.

2 Write a message on the postcard.

Mum,

Having a good trip.

From

Bot xxx

To Mum,

Reading and writing

1 **Read the sentences from the story about Bot.**

Bot let go of the club.

He hit the moon rock.

It was a big hit.

Bot got out the moon rock
and his best golf club.

2 **Write the sentences in the
correct order.**

- Read what you have written
  and check the order is correct.
- Write a sentence to tell
  what Bot did next.

Check!

Have you used capital
letters and full stops?

Is your work in the
correct order?

1 **PAIR WORK. Retell the story of _Bot on the Moon_.**

2 **Draw a story map of Bot's trip to the moon. Show what happened between Blast off! and Bot's visit to the Moon Shop.**

3 **Draw a robot that you would like to have.**

- Give your robot a name.
- Write a sentence about what you would like it to be able to do.

1 Listen to a poem about the moon.

Mister Moon

Mister Moon looks out of the sky
And watches me with his big bright eye

And follows me wherever I go
Hello, Mister Moon! Hello!

Of all the children that he can see
Why does he choose to follow me?

And watch me with his eye so bright
Good night, Mister Moon! Good night!

by Grace Andreacchi

2 PAIR WORK. Read the poem with a partner. Write the rhyming words.

Thinking time

Which did you prefer, *Bot on the Moon* or *Mister Moon*? Why?

5 *Funny Fish*

1 **PAIR WORK. Look at the title page of the book below. Talk about the questions.**

Written by Michaela Morgan

Illustrated by Jon Stuart

- What kind of book do you think it might be?
- What colours are the fish?
- How many fish are there?

- Do you think the fish are friends?
- Why do you think that?

2 **Read page 42. Talk about what you think the rest of the story is going to be about.**

Funny Fish

Three funny fish were swimming in the sea.

One funny fish said, "Look at me!"

"I am bright and funny and red."

"I am the best fish here," it said.

Then a big fish came and
swish, swish, swish ...

That was the end of
the funny red fish.

Two funny fish were
swimming in the sea.

One funny fish said,
"Look at ME!

I am yellow –
as bright as the sun!"

Then the big fish came and ...
Yum, yum, yum!

One funny fish was
swimming in the sea.

It said,
"No one ever looks at me."

Then along came the big fish —
oh, dear me.

The funny fish said,
"He can't see me!

I can hide.
I can look like a stone,
so the big bad fish
leaves me alone!"

Reading and writing

1 PAIR WORK.
Look at the picture.

One funny fish said, "Look at me!"

- Which fish do you think said this?
- How does the picture help you to know which fish said this?

2 Take turns to read the story again.

3 Read the sentences. Write the sentences that are true.

- The fish were swimming in a pond.
- One fish was red.
- One fish was green.
- One fish hid under a stone.
- The big fish ate two fish.
- One fish was yellow like the sun.

Reading and writing

1 **PAIR WORK. Read the words in the box.**

red   clever   brown   bossy   shy   bright   funny   boastful   spotty

2 **Write the words in two lists. Copy the headings below.**

Words about the red fish	Words about the brown fish

3 **Use some of the words to complete the sentences. Write the sentences.**

- "I am _____ and _____" said the brown fish.
- "I am _____ and _____" said the red fish.

4 **Draw and label a picture of the red fish and the brown fish.**

5 **Write a sentence about the big fish.**

Remember!
Include information about what the fish looks like.

Reading and writing

1 **Look at the picture.**
Read the sentence.

The fish is red and yellow.

2 **Read the words in the box.**

red   blue   brown   white   purple   black   yellow   green

3 **Write the sentences. Use the words from the box.**

The flower is _____
and _____.

The owl is _____
and _____.

The bird is _____
and _____.

The butterfly is _____
and _____.

I am yellow –
as bright as the sun!

1 Use the sounds in the box to make words that rhyme
with 'bright'. Write the words in a list.

fr   l   f   n   s   m   r   t   fl

__+ ight

2 Use some of the words that you have made to complete
the sentences. Write the sentences.

• I switched on the
_____.

• The sun is very _____.

• I go to bed at _____.

• I hurt my _____ hand.

1 PAIR WORK. Read the poems out loud. Read them together and take turns to read them alone.

A Fine Feathered Fish

A fine feathered fish
With five furry fins
Falls onto a dish
Next to four fishy tins.

This fine feathered fish
With five furry fins
Yells "Quick!" to those fish
"Come out of those tins!"

One, two, three, four, five

One, two, three, four, five
Once I caught a fish alive.
Six, seven, eight, nine, ten
Then I let it go again.

Why did you let it go?
Because it bit my finger so.

Reading and writing

1 Choose the correct words from the poems to complete the sentences. Copy the sentences.

- The fish falls onto a _____. (dish, tin)
- The fish has _____ (furry, hairy) fins.
- There are _____ (four, five) fishy tins.
- It bit _____ finger so! (me, my)

2 PAIR WORK. Use the frameworks below to make up nonsense rhymes.

A funny old fish in a hat and a coat
Went for a sail _____.

The funny old fish had a bump on his head
He put on a plaster _____.

3 Choose your favourite from the three rhymes. Write the rhyme and draw a picture.

Thinking time

Which fish from the three rhymes would you prefer to be and why?

6 Food

Listening and speaking

PAIR WORK. Look at the poster. Talk about the questions.

- Where might you see a poster like this?
- How many food groups are there?
- What food is in each group?

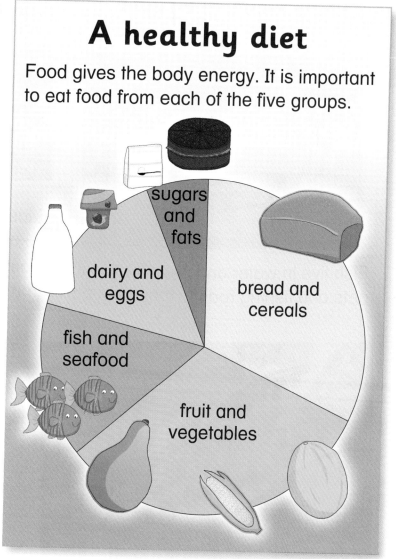

A healthy diet

Food gives the body energy. It is important to eat food from each of the five groups.

sugars and fats

dairy and eggs

bread and cereals

fish and seafood

fruit and vegetables

Writing

Copy and complete the sentences.

Food gives us _____.

We should eat food from _____.

PAIR WORK. Read about fish and seafood.

Fish and seafood

Fish live in water and people use nets and fishing rods to catch them.

Most fish live wild in rivers, lakes and the sea.
Some fish that we eat come from fish farms.

There are many different types of fish.

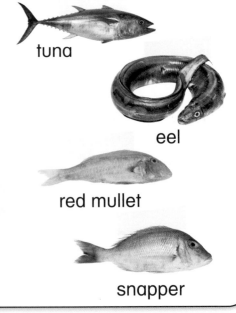

tuna

eel

red mullet

snapper

There are lots of other things from the sea that we can eat.

Reading and writing

Copy and complete the sentences.

- Fish live in _____.
- Most fish live in _____, _____ and _____ _____.
- People catch fish with _____ _____ and _____.

> **Remember!**
> We link parts of sentences with joining words like 'and' and 'or'.

Listening and speaking

PAIR WORK. Look at the pictures. Read the words out loud. Take turns to choose one and describe it.

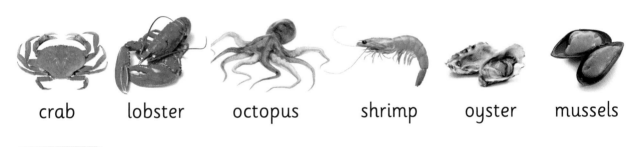

crab   lobster   octopus   shrimp   oyster   mussels

Writing

Draw three types of seafood and label them.

Listening and speaking

PAIR WORK. Talk about the questions.

- Do you eat fish and seafood?
- Is fish and seafood eaten cooked or uncooked?

1 PAIR WORK. Read about fruit and vegetables.

Fruit and vegetables

banana   onions

Fruit and vegetables are healthy foods.
Fruit and vegetables are plants.

Some fruits grow on trees
and some fruits grow on vines.

grapes grow   mango
on vines   tree

Fruits have skins. Some fruits
have to be peeled before eating.

orange   lychee   watermelon

Some fruits have large stones
which cannot be eaten.

avocado   peach   mango

Vegetables are plants. We eat different parts of vegetable plants.

Onion and garlic
are bulb vegetables.

Carrots and radishes
are root vegetables.

Spinach and pak choi
are leaf vegetables.

2 Talk about fruit and vegetables.

- What fruit have you eaten and liked or disliked?
- What vegetables have you eaten and liked or disliked?

1 Copy and complete the sentences.

- Fruit and vegetables are _____ _____.
- Some fruits grow on _____ and some fruits grow on _____.
- Some fruits need to be _____ before we can eat them.
- Some fruits have large _____.

2 Draw and label each fruit.

- A fruit with a stone.
- A fruit with skin that can be eaten.
- A fruit with skin that cannot be eaten.

3 Copy and complete the sentences.

- Vegetables are _____.
- We eat different _____ of vegetable plants.

4 Draw some different kinds of vegetables.

- Draw a root vegetable.
- Draw a bulb vegetable.
- Draw a leaf vegetable.

5 Choose a fruit. Write three facts about it.

PAIR WORK. Read about dairy and eggs.

Dairy and eggs

Dairy foods contain milk. Most milk comes from cows. The cows go to a milking shed each day so the farmer can milk them.

A truck called a milk tanker takes the milk from the farm to a place called a dairy.

At the dairy the milk is heated to kill germs. Then it is put into bottles or cartons to be sold.

Different kinds of food are made from milk, such as cheese and butter.

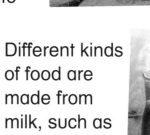

Cheese can also be made from goat's or sheep's milk.

Most eggs that we eat come from chickens.

Farmers collect the eggs and put them in boxes to sell.

Reading and writing

1 **Copy and complete the sentences.**

- Dairy foods are made from _____.
- Milk comes from _____.

2 **Draw a story map to show how we get milk to drink.**

3 **Write captions for your drawings.**

4 **Make a list of different kinds of food that are made from milk.**

5 **Copy and complete the sentences.**

- Most eggs we eat come from _____.
- Farmers collect the eggs and put them in _____ to _____.

6 **Ice cream is made from milk, cream, sugar and flavouring.**

- Draw a picture of a new ice cream that you would like.
- Make a list of the ingredients that you would need to make your ice cream.

7 **Draw a poster to advertise your ice cream.**

PAIR WORK. Read about bread and cereals.

Bread and cereals

Bread is made mostly of flour.

Flour is usually made from a kind of grass called wheat. Farmers grow wheat in fields.

There are lots of different kinds of bread.

baguette

croissant

People eat bread in countries all around the world.

pitta

People can make sandwiches with bread.

You can put lots of different foods in sandwiches.

challah

naan

People eat rice in countries all around the world.

Rice grows best in shallow water, in warm places. Rice fields are known as paddy fields.

Farmers stand in the water to cut down rice plants so they can collect the grains.

Rice can also be harvested by machines.

Reading and writing

① Copy and complete the sentences.

- Bread is made mostly of _____.
- Flour is made from _____.
- Farmers grow wheat in _____.

② Make a list of three different types of bread.

Listening and speaking

PAIR WORK. Talk about the questions.

- What do you need to make a sandwich?
- How do you make a sandwich?
- What do you like to put in a sandwich?

Reading and writing

Copy and complete the sentences.

- Rice plants grow in
  _____ _____.

- Rice fields are known as _____ _____.

Listening and speaking

PAIR WORK. Talk about the questions.

- How is rice cooked at home?
- What do you eat with rice?

1 Draw and label each of the fatty and sugary foods.
Use the words in the box to help.

cakes   sugary drinks   jam   biscuits   butter   chocolate   crisps

Sugars and fats

It is important not to eat too many of these types of foods.

2 Design a cover for a book about food.

3 Write a contents page for your food book.

Thinking time

Talk about the food you eat and enjoy. Is it always healthy food? What makes some food unhealthy?

7 Traditional stories

Reading and writing

**Look at the book cover.
Answer the questions.**

- What is the book called?
- What is the writer's name?
- Do you think this is a fiction or a non-fiction book? Give a reason for your answer.
- What do you think the book is going to be about? Give a reason for your answer.

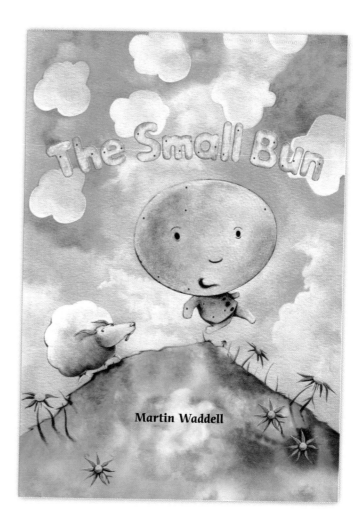

Listening and reading

**Listen to the story.
Think about the questions.**

- Who is the main character in the story?
- How many animal characters are in the story?
- What are their names?

The Small Bun

A hungry man baked a small bun. He sat down with his wife to eat the small bun but ...

... the small bun hopped off the dish and ran. Its little legs ran so fast that the bun got away.

The small bun met a hungry sheep by the gate.
"Lunch! Yummy-yum!" said the sheep.

"I am too fast for the man and his wife, and I am too fast for you!" said the bun.
Its little legs ran so fast that the bun got away.

5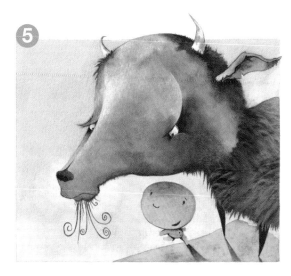

The small bun met a hungry goat in the lane.

"Stand still till I eat you!" said the goat.

6

"I am too fast for the man and his wife and the sheep, and I am too fast for you!" said the bun.

Its little legs ran so fast that the bun got away.

7

The small bun met a cunning fox by the river.

"What a plump little bun!" said the cunning fox, licking his lips.

8

"I am too fast for the man and his wife, and the sheep, and the goat, and I am too fast for you!" said the bun.

But ...

... the river was there.

The small bun was trapped!

It kept running about, with the fox running after it.

They ran so fast that they ran out of running and stopped.

"You have beaten me," the fox huffed and puffed. "Get on my back and I will carry you across the river."

"If I get on your back, you will eat me!" said the bun.

"Trust me," said the cunning fox.

The bun got on the back of the fox.

But the fox stopped in the middle of the river.

"Why have you stopped?" asked the bun.

"To eat you!" said the fox.

Gulp! Yum, yum, yum!

And that was the end of the bun.

1 **PAIR WORK. Take turns to read the story.**

2 **Draw a picture of each animal in the story.**

3 **Write the name of each animal under its picture.**

4 **Answer the questions.**

- Who baked the bun?
- How many people sat at the table?
- What happened after they sat down?
- How do you think they felt?

Sounds and spelling

1 **Look at the pictures. Say the words for each picture. What sound do you hear in the middle of each word?**

Sound it out

Two letters.
One sound: ee.

- Write the letters that make the sound in the middle of each word.

- Practise joining the two letters.

Word book

Write the words with 'ee' in your Word Book.

2 **Say the words for each picture. What sound do you hear at the end of each word?**

- Write the words.

3 **Copy and complete the sentences.**

- The _____ has green leaves.

- A _____ makes honey.

- The number after two is _____.

1 **Look at the pictures. Say the word for each picture. What sound do you hear in the middle of each word?**

- Write the letters that make the sound.
- Can you join the two letters? Practise joining the two letters.
- Write the words.

Sound it out

Two letters.
One sound: oa.

2 **Read the words in the box. Write the pairs of words that rhyme.**

road   coast   goal   soak   cloak   foal   toast   toad

3 **Use the letters in the boxes to make lists of rhyming words.**

c   b   m

_____ oat

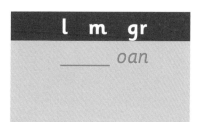

l   m   gr

_____ oan

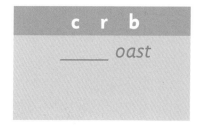

c   r   b

_____ oast

Reading and writing

1 **Read the words in the box.**

my   you   have   me

- Write each word three times.

2 **Use the words in question 1 to complete and copy the sentences.**

- You _____ beaten me.
- Get on _____ back.
- Trust _____.
- To eat _____!

3 **Read the story starters.**

- A long time ago…
- Long ago and far away…
- Once upon a time…
- Once there was…

Choose a story starter. Write the first sentence of a story.

1 **Read the recipe for buns.**

Recipe for buns

Ingredients

eggs   sugar   butter   flour

Method

- Put the tray in the oven.
- Leave the buns to cool.
- Mix the ingredients well.
- Take the tray out of the oven when the buns are ready.
- Put the mixture on to a baking tray.

Check!
When you have written out the recipe, read it aloud to make sure it makes sense.

2 **Write the recipe in the correct order. Use the pictures below to help you.**

Reading and writing

1 **Write the names of the characters in the story.**

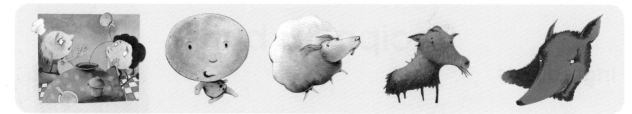

2 **Read the sentence below the picture.
Think about the questions.**

The small bun hopped off the dish and ran.

- What do you think the man might have said when the bun ran away?
- What do you think the woman might have said when the bun ran away?

3 **Draw a story map of the small bun's meeting with the sheep, the goat and the fox.**

4 **Write captions under the pictures.**

Thinking time

How could the hungry man and his wife show their feelings without speaking?

8 Feelings

PAIR WORK. Look at the book cover. Talk about it. What do you think the book is about?

- Read the title.
- Look at the picture.

Speaking and reading

1 PAIR WORK. Talk about why the penguin might be lonely.

2 Take turns to read the story.

3 Talk about why the penguin was lonely.

The Lonely Penguin

1

Crunch crunch! Who's coming through the snow?

2

It's Penguin. He's lonely.

3

Crunch crunch! Penguin's looking for his friends.

4

He can't think where they can be.

5

Crunch crunch! Penguin's running through the snow.

6

He's sliding on the frosty ice.

7

Crunch crunch!
Penguin's looking everywhere.

8

Penguin climbs up the hill.
Are his friends at the top?

9

No. Penguin looks down into the sea. Are his friends at the bottom?

Penguin jumps into the air.

10

SPLASH!

11

Yes! Penguin finds his friends swimming in the cold water.

12

They all laugh and say, "Where have you been?"

1 **Choose the sentence to match each picture.**
Write the sentence.

Penguin is looking for his friends.

Penguin is running through the snow.

Penguin finds his friends.

Penguin is running through the snow.

Penguin is looking everywhere.

Penguin is sliding on the frosty ice.

Penguin looks down into the sea.

Penguin climbs up the hill.

2 **Look at the sentences above.**

- How many words are in the first sentence?
- How many sentences are there about penguins?

Reading and writing

Crunch, crunch!
Who's coming through the snow?

1 **Find words ending with –*ing* in**
The Lonely Penguin.
Write the page number
and the word like this.

Page 1   coming

2 **Add –*ing* to make**
new words.
Write the new words.
Read the words aloud.

look	fish
keep	cook
crash	peep
hook	brush
sleep	

3 **Write the sentences. Use the words from the box.**

swimming   running   sliding

- Penguin is _____ on the frosty ice.
- Penguin is _____ in the cold water.
- Penguin is _____ through the snow.

Sounds and spelling

Penguin wanted to find his friends.
He went to look for them.

1 Say the word 'look'. What sound do you hear in the middle of the word?

- Write the letters that make the sound in the middle of the word 'look'.
- Can you join the two letters? Practise joining the two letters.
- Quickly write the word 'look' three times.

2 Look at the pictures. Say the word for each picture.

Word book

Write the words from question 2 in your Word book.

3 Use the letters in the boxes to make lists of rhyming words.

h l st

_____ oop

c t st p

_____ ool

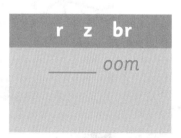

r z br

_____ oom

PAIR WORK. Retell the story of *The Lonely Penguin*.

Reading and writing

❶ Draw a story map of the lonely penguin looking for his friends, like the one below.

Start with the lonely penguin running through the snow and finish when he finds his friends.

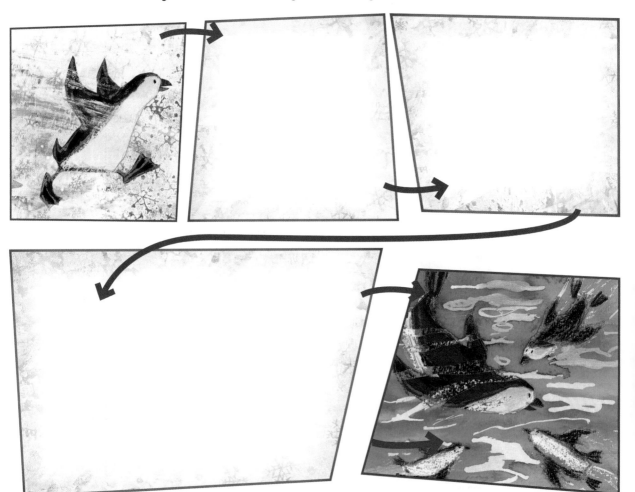

❷ Write some captions under the pictures.

PAIR WORK. Read the fact file about penguins.

FACT FILE: Penguins

Penguins are birds that do not fly.

Penguins are good swimmers.

Penguins use their WINGS as flippers.

Penguins eat fish and other small sea creatures.

Penguins can drink seawater.

Larger penguins live in colder climates and smaller penguins live in warmer climates.

The emperor penguin is the tallest penguin.

The little blue penguin is the smallest type of penguin.

A baby penguin is called a chick.

Reading and writing

1 **Read about penguins in the fact file on page 79 again.**

2 **Write the sentences that are true.**

- Penguins are birds.
- Penguins can fly.
- Penguins can swim.
- A baby penguin is called a cub.
- Penguins eat plants.
- The smallest penguin is the little blue.

3 **Answer the questions**

- What do penguins eat?
- What do penguins use to help them swim?
- What do penguins drink?
- What is the largest type of penguin?
- What is a baby penguin called?

Time to think

Which text did you prefer – the story about the penguin or the fact file about real penguins? Why?

9 Life lessons

Listen to the story. Follow the words.

Anansi and Turtle

Anansi the spider sat down
to dinner.
There was a loud knock on
the door.
Anansi did not like visitors at
dinner time. He did not want to
share his food with guests.

Anansi opened the door and
there was his friend Turtle.

"Mmm! What a lovely smell.
Can I join you for dinner?"
asked Turtle.

"Of course," said Anansi.

"Oh Turtle, your hands are dirty.
You cannot eat food with dirty
hands," said Anansi.
"I had a long walk to get here,
that is why my hands are dirty.
I will go and wash them,"
replied Turtle.

"Turtle walks slowly," thought
Anansi. "I have time to eat."
"Yum, yum, rice and beans, sweet
potatoes, beef and dumplings,"
said Anansi.
Anansi began to eat, stuffing
food into his mouth.

When Turtle returned, he saw that the plates were empty. "Why did you not wait for me?" asked Turtle. "You were too slow and I was hungry," answered Anansi. Turtle left with an empty tummy.

When Turtle got home, he thought, "Anansi tricked me. I must teach him a lesson."

Invitation
To : Anansi
Please come to dinner.
Place : At the pond
Time : 5 o'clock
From : Turtle

Next day, Anansi found an invitation in his mailbox.

Anansi put on his best coat and hat, and set off to the pond where Turtle lived.

Turtle had set the table at the bottom of the pond. All of Anansi's favourite foods – jerk chicken, rice and peas, and sweet coconut drops were piled on the table.

"Come down," shouted Turtle.

Anansi jumped into the water, but he did not sink.

"I know," said Anansi, "I will fill my coat pockets with stones. That will help me sink to the bottom."

Glug! Glug! Glug! Anansi went to the bottom of the pond.

"Wait. Remember your manners Anansi," said Turtle. "You must not eat dinner with your hat and coat on."

Anansi took his hat and coat off. He floated to the top of the water.

Anansi climbed out of the pond. He stood at the edge and watched Turtle eat all the scrumptious food.

"This time, Turtle has tricked me," he sighed.

Reading and writing

1 Read pages 1 to 4 of the story. Write the names of the characters.

2 Read the sentences. Write the ones that are true.

- Anansi stuffed food into his mouth.
- Anansi had good manners.
- Anansi had just finished his dinner when Turtle knocked on the door.
- There was plenty of food on Anansi's table to share.
- Anansi's hands were dirty.
- Turtle walked to Anansi's house.

3 Say the words in these sentences in the correct order.

- on loud door. was knock There a the
- of the water. to the top He floated
- out He pond. the climbed of

Remember

A sentence starts with a capital letter.

4 Write the sentences correctly.

5 Read the words in the box.

> greedy   mean   kind   generous   hungry

- Draw a picture of Anansi.
- Write his name under the picture.
- Write a list of words to describe Anansi. Use some of the words in the box to help you.

1 **PAIR WORK. Read the whole story.**

- Talk about how Turtle felt when he arrived at Anansi's house. Write the sentences that make you think this.

- Talk about what happened when Turtle arrived at Anansi's house. Write the sentences that make you think this.

2 **Read page 4 again.**

- Write a list of the food that Anansi ate. Start like this:
  Anansi's food
  - rice
  -

- Write a list of food that you would give a friend coming to dinner. Write a heading for your list.

- Turtle was hungry when he left Anansi's house. Write the sentence that tells you this.

3 **Read the words in the box.**

| sad | happy | upset | tearful | joyful | angry |

- Draw a picture of Turtle. Write his name under the picture.

- Write a list of words to describe Turtle when he left Anansi's house. Use the words in the box to help you.

1 **Look at the picture. Read the words.**

"Why did you not wait for me?" asked Turtle.

- Find the word 'why'.
- Say the word 'why' aloud.
- What sound do you hear at the end of the word 'why'?
- Write the word 'why' three times.

2 **Use the letters in the box to make a list of words that rhyme with 'why'.**

m   cr   b   dr   tr
fl   sp   sk   sh

m + y   my
cr + y   cry

Word book

Write the words in your Word book.

3 **PAIR WORK. Read your partner's list of words.**

- Talk about the words.
- Check that you know what each word means.

4 **Choose two words. Write a sentence for each word.**

Reading and writing

❶ Read the sentences about Anansi.

Anansi opened the door and there was his friend, Turtle.

Yum, yum, rice and beans, sweet potatoes, beef and dumplings.

- Find the nouns in the sentences.
- Write the nouns in a list.

❷ Read the sentences about Anansi's food.

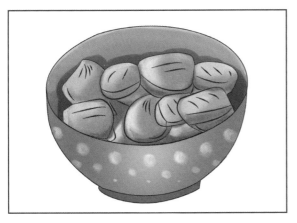 

Anansi liked beef and dumplings.

Anansi liked rice and beans.

- Write two sentences about what you like to eat.
  Start your sentences with the word 'I'.
  Use the word 'and' in both sentences.

Reading, speaking and writing

❶ PAIR WORK. Read the poem out loud with a partner. Then read it to each other.

Myrtle and Merlin
And Matty MacMouse
Make a marvellous meal
In their mini mouse house.

They mix it with mushrooms
And marigolds too.
They melt it in the moonlight
To make a magical stew.

"The most marvellous meal
For ravenous mice,"
Says Mummy MacMouse,
"Mmmm! So yummy, so nice!"

❷ Answer the questions.

- How many characters are in the poem?
- Where are the mice?

❸ Find and write:

- the names of two of the characters.
- the name of one ingredient.
- two rhyming words.
- two nouns.
- two verbs.

Listening and speaking

PAIR WORK.

- Use the pictures to retell this part of the story.
- Imagine one of you is Anansi and the other is Turtle. What do you think they say? Act out what happens.

Check!
Try to show how your character feels by the way you stand and the gestures you use as well as your words.

Speaking and writing

PAIR WORK.

- What might have happened when Anansi went to visit Turtle? Talk about a different ending for the story.
- Write your new ending for the story. Remember to use capital letters and full stops.

PAIR WORK. Talk about the questions.

- What way did Anansi behave in the story?
- What way did Turtle behave at the beginning of the story?
- What way did Turtle behave in the second part of the story?
- Do you think this was the correct way to behave? Why?

Thinking time

Which was your favourite text in this book? Why?

Text acknowledgements
The publishers gratefully acknowledge the permissions granted to reproduce copyright material in the book. Every effort has been made to contact the holders of copyright material, but if any have been inadvertently overlooked, the Publisher will be pleased to make the necessary arrangements at the first opportunity.

Cover illustration: *The Lonely Penguin* Reprinted by permission of HarperCollins*Publishers* Ltd © 2011 Petr Horácek. *The Big Red Bus* Reprinted by permission of HarperCollins*Publishers* Ltd © 2006 Alison Hawes, illustrated by Woody Fox; *Pet Cat, Big Cat* Reprinted by permission of HarperCollins*Publishers* Ltd © 2006 Alison Hawes; *Animal Coats* Reprinted by permission of HarperCollins*Publishers* Ltd © 2011 Clare Llewellyn; *Best Bird* HarperCollins*Publishers* Ltd © 2011 Laura Hambleton; *In the Forest* Reprinted by permission of HarperCollins*Publishers* Ltd © 2011 Becca Heddle; *Bot on the Moon* Reprinted by permission of HarperCollins*Publishers* Ltd © 2006 Shoo Rayner; *Funny Fish* Reprinted by permission of HarperCollins*Publishers* Ltd © 2005 Michaela Morgan, illustrated by Jon Stuart; *The Small Bun* Reprinted by permission of HarperCollins*Publishers* Ltd © 2006 Martin Waddell, illustrated by T. S. Spookytooth; *The Lonely Penguin* Reprinted by permission of HarperCollins*Publishers* Ltd © 2011 Petr Horácek.

We are grateful to the following for permission to reproduce copyright material:
Coolabi Group Ltd for the poem on p.30 'Lion' from *Rumble in the Jungle* written by Giles Andreae and illustrated by David Wojtowycz, Tiger Tales, 2001, text copyright © Purple Enterprises Limited 2016; Grace Andreacchi for the poem on p.40 'Mister Moon' from *Little poems for children* copyright © Grace Andreacchi; and Joyce Vallar for the poem on p.49 'A Fine Feathered Fish' by Joyce Vallar from *Hector Hedgehog's Big Book of Rhymes*, Collins Fun Phonics, copyright © Joyce Vallar.

Photo acknowledgements
The publishers wish to thank the following for permission to reproduce photographs. Every effort has been made to trace copyright holders and to obtain their permission for the use of copyright materials. The publishers will gladly receive any information enabling them to rectify any error or omission at the first opportunity.

(t = top, c = centre, b = bottom, r = right, l = left)

p10tl Picture Partners/Alamy Stock Photo, p10tr Yann Arthus-Bertrand/Corbis, p10c Sergey Uryadnikov/Dreamstime, p10b Photoshot/Alamy Stock Photo, p21l Photoshot/Alamy Stock Photo, p21b Sergey Uryadnikov/Dreamstime, p21tr Picture Partners/ Alamy Stock Photo, p21tr Yann Arthus-Bertrand/Corbis, p22l Martin Mcmillan/Dreamstime, p22r Heikki Mäkikallio/Dreamstime, p24tl Graham Chalmers/ImageState/Alamy Stock Photo, p24tr Tom Mackie/Alamy Stock Photo, p24bl Gianpiero Ferrari/ FLPA, p24bl Cyril Ruoso/BiosPhoto, p24c Wildchromes/Alamy Stock Photo, p24r Juniors Bildarchiv GmbH/Alamy Stock Photo, p25 Vladimir Chernyanskiy/Shutterstock, p26tl Pim Leijen/Shutterstock, p26tcl yevgeniy11/Shutterstock, p26tcr Pan Xunbin/ Shutterstock, p26tr TTstudio/Shutterstock, p26bl Yanik Chauvin/Shutterstock, p26cr Jamie Hall/Shutterstock, p26br Vladimir Chernyanskiy/Shutterstock, p27bl wong yu liang/Shutterstock, p27bc, br Eric Isselee/Shutterstock, p28cl, tcl, tcr, bcl, br Eric Isselee/ Shutterstock, p28bcr photomaster/Shutterstock, p30t Ludmila Yilmaz/Shutterstock, p30b ESB Professional/Shutterstock, p35 MarcelClemens, p37 Hugo Felix/Shutterstock, p52tl Gail Palethorpe/Shutterstock, p52tr CHEN WS/Shutterstock, p52cl holbox/ Shutterstock, p52ltc Azdora/Shutterstock, p52rbc Evlakhov Valeriy/Shutterstock, p52br Evlakhov Valeriy/Shutterstock, p52bl lupu robert ciprian/Shutterstock, p53l Ozgur Coskun/Shutterstock, p53rrc, cl JIANG HONGYAN/Shutterstock, p53rc rangizzz/ Shutterstock, p53llc Edward Westmacott/Shutterstock, p53r Angorius/Shutterstock, p55 bluecrayola/Shutterstock, p56tr Wasan Srisawat/Shutterstock, p56btr Pavel L Photo and Video/Shutterstock, p56lc Degtiarova Viktoriia/Shutterstock, p56rc Silberkorn/ Shutterstock, p56bl Celiafoto/Shutterstock, p56br TTstudio/Shutterstock, p57t Elena Schweitzer/Shutterstock, p57b M. Unal Ozmen/Shutterstock, p58l Orientaly/Shutterstock, p58r stockphoto-graf/Shutterstock, p58r cristi180884/Shutterstock, p58r MidoSemsem/Shutterstock, p58r S1001/Shutterstock, p58r Richard Griffin/Shutterstock, p58l dotshock/Shutterstock, p58br MOSO IMAGE/Shutterstock, p59t Shebeko/Shutterstock, p59b Karramba Production/Shutterstock, p60tr Nattika/Shutterstock, p60 Sergey Skleznev/Shutterstock, p60tc SuriyaPhoto/Shutterstock, p60cr Yalcin Sonat/Shutterstock, p60tl makeitdouble/Shutterstock, p60br Moving Moment/Shutterstock, p60bl Multiart/Shutterstock, p68 NextMarsMedia/Shutterstock, p69r M. Unal Ozmen/Shutterstock, p69l Nattika/Shutterstock, p69cl fotogiunta/Shutterstock, p69cr Multiart/Shutterstock, p79tr Christian Musat/Shutterstock, p79cl Stanislav Fosenbauer/Shutterstock, p79cr bikeriderlondon/Shutterstock, p79bl Khoroshunova Olga/Shutterstock, p79br Roger Clark ARPS/Shutterstock, p88 Sasha Mosyagina/Shutterstock.